JESUS WAS A KID, JUST LIKE ME

Cynthia Arent

ISBN: 0692899219
ISBN 13: 9780692899212

This book belongs to:

_____

Jesus got dressed,
Just like me.

Jesus ate breakfast,
Just like me.

Jesus went to school,
Just like me.

Jesus played with friends,
Just like me.

Jesus got boo-boos,
Just like me.

Jesus helped Mommy,
Just like me.

Jesus had family,
Just like me.

Jesus learned about God,
Just like me.

Jesus went to bed,
Just like me.

Jesus was a kid,
Just like me.

www.ingramcontent.com/pod-product-compliance
Lightning Source LLC
Chambersburg PA
CBHW040347060426
42445CB00029B/38